Yip Is in the Cubs!

By Sally Cowan

Yip and Mum went
to see the Cubs.

Yip is not in the Cubs yet.

Yip's bat is in his bag.

He did up the zip.

Six kids are in the Cubs.

Reb looks and looks.

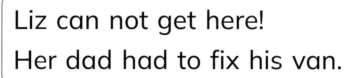
Liz can not get here!
Her dad had to fix his van.

"Tex!" said Reb.

"Yip can bat!"

Reb did a big hit!

She ran and ran.

Yip did a big, **big** hit!

Run, Yip! Run!
The Cubs can win!

"Can Yip be in the Cubs, too?" said Reb.

Yes!

CHECKING FOR MEANING

1. What did Yip have in his bag? *(Literal)*

2. How many children are in the Cubs? *(Literal)*

3. Who did the bigger hit, Reb or Yip? *(Inferential)*

EXTENDING VOCABULARY

yet	What does *yet* mean in *Yip is not in the Cubs yet*? Does this mean Yip may be in the Cubs one day? If you take away the *y* at the start of the word, what other letter could you put there to make a new word?
zip	What is a *zip*? Is this the short form of a longer word? What is the longer word? If you change the first letter of *zip* to the letter *l*, what is the new word?
fix	How many sounds are in this word? What are they? How many other words can you make by taking away the letter *f* and putting another letter at the start?

MOVING BEYOND THE TEXT

1. Why did Mum go with Yip when he went to the Cubs?
    How do you think Yip was feeling?

2. Why was Reb worried when Liz wasn't there?
    Do you think Liz is a good player?

3. What do you have to do when you are playing in a
    team that you don't have to do when you are playing
    a game by yourself?

4. Why do you like being in a team?

SPEED SOUNDS

PRACTICE WORDS

yet

Yip

six

Yes

zip

Liz

fix

Tex